OUR FOREIGNER

BOOKS BY NANCE VAN WINCKEL

Visual Poetry
Book of No Ledge

Poetry
Pacific Walkers

No Starling

Beside Ourselves

After A Spell

A Measure of Heaven

The Dirt

Bad Girl, with Hawk

The 24 Doors: Advent Calendar Poems

Fiction
Ever Yrs

Boneland

Curtain Creek Farm

Quake

Limited Lifetime Warranty

OUR FOREIGNER

Poems

Nance Van Winckel

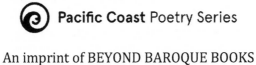

Pacific Coast Poetry Series

An imprint of BEYOND BAROQUE BOOKS

Our Foreigner

Pacific Coast Poetry Series
An imprint of Beyond Baroque Books
ISBN: 978-1-892184-08-5

Cover Design
Joanne Minerbi

Cover Painting
Inamorata in Sheep's Clothing
By Tyson Grumm

Beyond Baroque Literary Arts Center
681 Venice Boulevard
Venice, CA, 90291

·

310-822-3006
www.beyondbaroque.org

Pacific Coast Poetry Series

ACKNOWLEDGEMENTS

Thanks to the editors of the journals in which these poems (some in slightly different versions) first appeared:

Agni: "Brought to Us By"

American Poetry Review: "In the Moment" and "Stateside, 1972"

Beloit Poetry Journal: "Given Unto Ye"

Cincinnati Review: "To the El" and "Talk-Talk, Ambulance Style"

Crazyhorse: "And the Wound Says," "Eat *This*," and "Rubbing the Scar Away"

Field: "One Must Divorce Oneself," "When He Snaps His Fingers," "Lest You Forget: Cake Never Comes Before the Prayers," "The Thing Is," and "Unsigned Letter"

Gettysburg Review: "Denied Your Heaven, We Shall Deny You Ours" and "The Four Third Cousins (Annual Visit)"

Green Mountains Review: "Larder"

Handsome Journal: "Dear Deer"

Idaho Review: "Snowshoe Thompson & the Mail"

The Journal: "Hit Return"

Kenyon Review: "I Leaned Over the Railing"

The Massachusetts Review: "Casting the Wrong Shadows"

New England Review: "The Object of the Object" and "In the Old Man's Favorite Soap Opera"

Ploughshares: "Volunteer"

Poetry: "Nest," "Crypts" and "The Apophatic"

Prairie Schooner: "The Red Line" and "Missive"

Southern Poetry Review: "Left to Our Own Devices" and "Of No Use"

Southern Review: "Only a Speck in the Mind, But It Was Burning" and "Coxswain"

Third Coast: "The Hearse Broke Free"

West Branch: "Click on Any Image to Enlarge Her" and "A Man Comes Down"

CONTENTS

I. The Object of the Object

II. Fold

III. To the Far North

IV. In the Moment

V. Cold Interiors

Thare were a great many wagons gone with that man and thare a great many more going and we thought if it was a nearer and better road we had as much need to go as anybody well on we went . . .

—from a letter written by Elizabeth Stewart Warner in 1865.
Women's Diaries of the Westward Journey
Schocken Books, New York, 1982

OUR FOREIGNER

I. The Object of the Object

GIVEN UNTO YE

I came upon the vast maybe in the dark—
a match struck, the light flickering,
and the proffered books set before me
were red, leather-bound, and each
smaller than a demitasse saucer.

But how riveting
the stories therein. I turned pages
with my pinkie nail, inquiring of
the invisible bestower, Mightn't I
peruse the whole set first? So hard
to choose just one.

It was a poor light,
but it was mine for the night
and a night had been all
I'd been granted.

A Man Comes Down

A man coming down the mountain no longer
remembers the way to town. His dog barely
knows him. I'm supposed to meet him, supposed
to tell him his daughter's arthritic, fat as a berry,
flat as a boy. His son's a scraggly Christ case
in the asylum. I'm supposed to remind him
the dog's name is Wolf, and a jug of rye
waits under the old stump—if
the marmots haven't got there first.

I'm to say no one blames you. A thousand
thousand years, and he's plodding down
with just the one stone tablet, which does
appear heavy, and which, Hey, maybe
you want to set that thing down.

I'm supposed to give you this walking stick.
Yes, the slope, in our era, has indeed
steepened. Okay, we'll say it's not your fault
sleep loved you too well and too long
and that your wife—three centuries ago—
quit stripping threads from her loom.

No, no one eats meat anymore. Yes, you do
look like something a whale's spit up,
like you're here to say big things, but sure
when you're wider awake. Right, the tiny horses
are extinct now, and it is, truly, a shame. We all
loved them. Of course you aren't to blame.

To have spent a life in a dream and not once
felt hail scoring hits on your head. . . well,
frankly, a lot's never added up. Rumors you
finally bored stiff the Sirens and the Cyclops.
And how odd you've come down still
dressed in the ratty furs you wore up.

True, the marmots often act tipsy like this.
Yeah, it seems everyone's had quite a night here,
some party. Don't worry. You *were* missed
for a few weeks. I'm supposed to tell you
to be prepared, there may be no one
home in your home, or no one
who loves you. There is only me, and I
am no one. I am just the messenger.

THUNDERBIRDS RIDING THE THUNDERHEAD

We woke and had
to hurry. Oaths
had been prepared
by the one who insists
we salute. We do; we will.

And with nary enough time
to read the leather-bound
manual, only the odd
moment to stroke its
embossed silver letters,
our blanketed nude selves
are dressed and carted off.

Awake, I'm aware of a duty
for today: take the temperature
of the compost. Asleep,
I'd been sure we'd wake
as two blue flowers
in a crystal vase.

THE RED LINE

The Mommy says her Little Man eats, page by page,
whatever romance she's reading. Eats headlines
and bugs from the yard. The train rattles around us
and every time the doors blow apart, Little Man leans
to lick the breeze. He leaves no unturned stone
uneaten; every one's been fire-roasted, taste-tested.

When the oxygen tank, with its half-pint lady attached,
rolls aboard, Little Man reaches for that too—wondrous
airy meal. He nibbles at my grudge, then polishes off
my petulant shrug. What amplification he gives space
when his mouth opens. He may be one part per trillion
of the world, but he plans to ingest the other 999.9
billion. He has the stomach for it, for the hatless
or the hatted, for their paragraphs of dashed hopes.

The stops yank us out, pull us in. Little cloud
in Little Man's eye is all that makes him sleep,
and sleep on him is almost too terrible a beauty
to behold, although even asleep, Little Man punches
the Mommy's breast he's so sure will never empty, sure
he'll always stay a bee upon the white flower.

EAT *THIS*

Target cake with a looming bull's eye.
Tiered cake with dancing girl inside.
Called up, put upon—sisters, can we
bring one? A consecrated cake of sand
that ticks like a clock. Can we bake it
and box it and get it there by dawn?
Cake of the coming Zeitgeist, cake
that inches palely toward the timer's
ding. Watch the cakes that follow caskets,
the ones that honor cretins and despots.
Here comes the mink cake in its fox fur box;
there goes the one with a small fire inside,
the one with gilt letters rising at the edge
of blue frosting, and our favorite: soft
and moist and with a baked-in steel file.
Soon we'll need companion cakes, cake
indices, and a boy to fan away the gnats.
Cakes atop cakes until we expire upon
our mountain of crumbs. God help us
cool on a rack, bask on a sill. Try this cake
with a meadow inside. God bless
a cake that goes forth as prime provision
for covert passage. God spare us
bakers. Let the cake's sweetness
beguile its eaters.

OF NO USE

The amber-spotted deer step out at dusk. Here
    their trails long ago
        became cow paths, which later
        became the roads
that are slowly beginning to belong again
    to a field. Just starting to cross it now—
    a few intrepid bucks.

         *   *   *

We'd stayed out of trouble our whole lives.
    Then, as promised, we were given
        a key to the city. To get there
we took the shortest route,
    thinking ourselves so clever
    to follow those deer.

We hadn't expected ruins. The books had pictures:
    Fountains! Gardens! Carts
    to meet one at the gate.

         *   *   *

Those books: an inky cursive smoke of them
    hovers over the city. And that key—now
    it's what we use to poke the fire.

Duplicate Key

The drill bites. Configures
to what's prefigured
the route in. Pay, raise
a paw, & go. A bit of drool
aside, you look good
in dog years. With its
weird & sad & uninspired
activities, the brain
grinds on. Eating
without thinking. Or
a gaze at locked doors
to gather the inferences.
No more encores of
lifetimes. How completely
the loud majority lap
that shit up. The One-
Fine-Day-I-Will-Return.
Isn't it what the lover
tells the beloved—after
he's already sipped
from the poisoned cup?

The Thing Is

the iron valve's been

shut off so hard,

it's henceforth

unopenable. The thing

is bottom-drawered. You'd

been its tourist

and now it's yours.

Its frosted curlicues

burnished. Monochromed

by memory. What

was it called? Earth's

best guess goes in

on top. Hunkers

down. The thing is

the thing was

something

in its day.

THE OBJECT OF THE OBJECT

: to bound, or be
boundless. To be full
of itself, no longer

substitute for what
the eye prefers
to eat. To be meadow

at one end of the world,
money at the other,
unbitten by the body

between. To be
empty, an O
for zero, always

a portal, never
the port. Hiccup,
not horizon. No

figment of, no
sty in the eye of
the end of a page.

II. Fold

CRYPTS

Little cartons—objects I'd ordered—went on
biding time in the mailbox. I'd have to boot up
and go get them. The cold out there
pressing in. I could feel myself
        belonging some day to a box too:
            roughed-up bone dust

            as the Dog Star bears down,
        getting used to me—the nothing
    anyone opens happily.

Let the snowplow flash its light
and make a path this way
and away. Who will take
the path?
        No one.

    No one I shall see. Ah,
        all the same to me.

The Whitest White in the Black & White Movie

The murders, the heists,
      the rapidly heaving breasts
           reel up behind me.

An actor I've casually loved
      for an hour
           opens one eye

and I stare into the moment
      that's a stand-in
           for a lifetime.

With what sweet abandon
      he's still leaving himself

even as I re-enter
      at point-blank range

the tundra terrain
      of the body.

I Leaned Over the Railing

and was quite
awake. A fierce-minded
down-below.

The tilted jonquils—some
you'd plucked for me
in a by-gone not-bad year—

were set in this same light
dimmed by fledgling shadows
in which a dog or a deer

rears up. Oh that *it*
I'd been straining to see.
Before.

Before the above. Before
a proverbial hell
broke loose.

TALK-TALK, AMBULANCE STYLE

No, the snow did *not* burn you. Let's try
another mask. What ABC of your late day
brings you to the way back of our way back?
Remove the mask and you won't breathe.
Sure, the mysteries intersect at this stoplight
but we always run it, Honey. We're closing in
on the get-well-factory. Or possibly the *well* you
hasn't been invented yet? Try this mask then
over that other. "Miasmal Mist?" Those ain't
words we know. Breathe good or breathe bad
but breathe, Christ on a crutch, no talk, only
listen. It got close to but didn't strike bone.
Here's the heart then. Just. Just listen.
"Blue swallow?" No, no, blue pill.

AND THE WOUND SAYS

Step into the river and let the ripples cool us.
The spawned-out salmon, a few days
discreetly dead, are a mediocre meal
for the gulls. Look away.

I've ridden you, and you me,
as far as we can ride. Recall
our old darts and dashes
between black trees—because
you believed watercress
bloomed up through the algae.

Don't cling. Don't try to resist.
Thorn in the quick of being, I am
what I am. Object of non-desire.
Nothing more pure.

Did you expect the throb
to throw a less delirious fit of welcome?

Kneel. Even as the freeze
rushes forth above,
so our heat grinds on below.

RUBBING THE SCAR AWAY

The itch gets its scratch.
    The clock tips, minutes spill.
      Flecks of flesh sloughed off
at last. Half a heart—scuff mark
where the world shoved back
    at what so carelessly shoved
      through it. The way I come
    round in my mind. A radio,
an open window, and a nuthatch
    taking flight when I change
      the station. Itch: the leash
    tugs. Scratch. A name tag
rattles beneath my chin.

HIT RETURN

Your flame—an eye
flown open—stopped me.
The thunderbolt not
so much. The mind-changes
and ditto the curfew
make as if to stop me.
Good tries. Old ties.
A wail wells up (from
the has-been baby) and
aims to but fails to
take me aback. What
may be gleaned from
this? The very inquiry
stops me: had I come
on foot? The injection only
slows me. You pull
the needle out, and I
go on, darling, on.

LEFT TO OUR OWN DEVICES

A vein opens. The ore gleams.
  I peek out from the fold
      of a dog-eared page.

          An old clock's laid open
      and I lift from a bowl the tiny tools
          I've seen all my life but have
              no idea how to use.

DEAR DEER

No one collects your carcass. I guess
        that's good. Mashed hoof in filigree
            of leaf-light. Fly-ridden rot
                becomes frozen rib taking root.
                    You bend, you warp, you go.
             June slips its noose over May, and on
        like that. Everything that's about to happen
      is on its way to you. As it is to me.
A dream. A run. A wake.

III. To the Far North

COXSWAIN

His silence grants us rowers
a rest. On bad nights we feel
the winds' bite. On good nights
they're a balm. What casually falls
casually arrives: remnants of
unnamed stars. His shout throws
a switch. The city flinches. Nearing
the headwaters, we turn. Desire
expands before us even as distance
extends behind. This crew, these
unsown seeds in a pod . . . floating—
in us are the woods.

MISSIVE

Impatient, alone in the sleek dark,
I chanted your name your name, thinking
soon, surely *soon* I'd be seized by you.
I'd be raised, opened . . . .

I'd been a thing sent forth. Passing across
hands, through fingers and machines. Stamped.
Shipped downtown, flown around, honked at,
walked to a door, and slipped through a slot.

I had the patience of centuries. I waited—
for the door to fly inward, for the small wind
that would rush me forward to greet you
as you, buoyed by bright light, stepped toward me.

THE FOUR THIRD COUSINS (ANNUAL VISIT)

The plastic lamb in the yard has lost
two legs. Or was it supposed
to be kneeling? Hadn't there once
been a manger? And that fake well
with the green bucket we weren't
to touch—was that gone too?

Inside, the cousin who cooks won't
come out of the kitchen. The one
who smokes also repairs umbrellas.

Maude has a tiny stunted hand that hangs
just below her shoulder. At 72, she's
the youngest and still sews dresses
for brides, insists on combing their hair
after it's mussed by the veils. Her little hand
passes the other one the comb.

The eldest lights candles. We sit
and the cousins stare at our family's blue
in my eyes. Then we nod, cover the biscuits,
and pray in our old Quaker silence.

THE LAST FAMILY ON EARTH

Hail had bent the tulips down. No more
living through others' lives as red wires
with occasional juice pumping
through. The fuck and linger, kiss
and go. The family of slumped
skeletons embrace under a dripping
glacier. Their dog that was. This ice
that is. First light in a slow decay.
The hail storm
I woke to, and my face without pity
in an old man's mirror as I take him
his toast. The scratch of indelible ink
through which I scowl, through which
I witness scowls and wait for what must
eventuate—as if perhaps it won't.
When I tell him the storm's a lot
of bluster, he nods a gleaming
white skull. Since a storm has no
patience, it makes us have it all.

IN THE OLD MAN'S FAVORITE SOAP OPERA

someone's always doing her husband in
with a hatpin, and every Thursday
there's a thunderstorm, which is how we
know it's Thursday. Impregnations rife
on Fridays. No one ever spills or trips
or pees. No one has pets. It's always stay
tuned and come back tomorrow
and an evening can last into next week
if it's a night of sexual paydirt.

If we hear an organ before the next
commercial, a seizure is imminent. We like
the scripted hysteria—high-pitched but lucid
wailing, and hairdos professionally mussed.

We're fond of the woman who's tried
to blast into space and the one who's bundled
her child's bones into a napkin.

And we pity the aged patriarch
who couldn't bring himself to glance in the coffin
and see that the woman there was *not* the wife,
and so week by week he grows more bitter—
napping in his ratty robe by the TV that always
shows a dangerous surf in the distance
or the same fire with the same three flames.
Never locusts nor cripples. Never a cold river,
a too-swift current. Never old soldiers
still trying to slog to shore.

ONLY A SPECK IN THE MIND BUT IT WAS BURNING

In Friday's episode, unconsoled by a fifth
marriage, Amber was about to lock the real priest
in the confessional so he'd have to hear
her out, but first she'd sipped
from the communion wine, which
my father guesses was laced with
whatever the fake priest had in that vial.

Amber's famous breasts heave splendidly
when she swoons, and we have a long
May weekend to speculate if she's truly
dead, and if so, what might be a befitting
sendoff. We suppose it should be set far
north . . . on a glacial lake. We have one
in mind. Two oarsmen should row her remains
to a tiny island, which they'll torch and leave
quickly. The fire's white-edged flames
will ebb to soft blue smoke by the time
the rowers return to shore.

He Never Crawled Before He Walked
(Christ Retablo)

Still, I'd caution against letting the kid
get down on all fours now
for whatever he claims is the reason.

I'm not certain, I'm no healer
but his jackal eyes seem in pursuit of
what's wounded, lost, scattered

from the tribe. I can't say
for sure, but he hardly seems
begotten by even the most
minimal mother-love. I'm not
a hundred percent, I'm no tea-leaf
reader, but he's a tall drink, he's big talk

and sick of grief and so many alms
sloughed off on him. The sea
was calm, I suppose. I guess it did

appear walkable. Still, I doubt he'd
arrive here from there. I'm no
authority, but I had the torn heart

and there came, there was
his hot tongue, licking.

TO THE EL

Sausage smell in an alleyway. Shopping carts
tow the limping, bleary-eyed down the blocks.
I travel in their wake, set my toes in their
snowy heel holes, me likewise muttering
about my country, its trumped-up sense
of itself: the big fat hero, how it soars in its
own mind which it wants to be my mind.

Stop. Wait. A woman stands inside her metal
walker. She can't budge it another inch. Here
come more hands. She shrugs. How unstuck
can we make her in the years' bleached
white litter? In the centuries' astral sludge?
I push and she swears and they tug, and no one
gets through the turnstile until she does.

Unsigned Letter

History with snow at its edges
whitens my hair. Marks me
as the youngsters' master for the hour
that precedes their mockery.
I remain. Truly. Since you
asked. Of whose childhood
were you once a fleeting guest?
You there at eye-level
with the bravado of big stogies.
Poses struck like matches.
Real losses in the guises
of real losers. Hiss, flare,
and the heart rasp hewn away.
All manner of zeroes—made
by a tongue punching through—
go on dissipating from your century
into mine. Ever yours. I remain.
Deepest gratitude. Sincerely.

IV. In the Moment

In the Moment

Clay jar with a darkening heart inside,
spilled salt, splayed trout too long
in the sun and no good now, no use
to anyone. *Mere details,* my father said. *I don't
want my life lived, like yours, in quatrains.*

On the hinge of huge possibilities
was a door the wind rattled open
and banged shut. *What else?* he said.
Calling from a room where at all hours
the sky is seen through a stained drape.

Pinpricks, stick-folk—we stood in position
around his bed the way we'd stand
around the coffin in the moment before
we bent and took hold.

Clock stutter, inconsolable wind—
all detail, all mere continuing.

THE HEARSE BROKE FREE

Uncle Al nabbed a leaf from the funeral wreath
and ate it. As my other uncles did the same,
the hearse began to move. Soon the mourners
had to run to keep up. Running made them
laugh at themselves—the ones out in front
in top hats. Then the hearse broke free
of its horses. It sped past the pulp mill,
somehow still negotiating tight curves.
It charged past the yellow yield sign,
up an off-ramp. It was hard to recall
for whom we'd cried before we stood
there chuckling in the street, and it crossed
our minds that whoever it was didn't expect
any more of our love anyway, which seemed
best, given how the hearse plunged now
past the mattress factory, past the fishery
and brewery, the uncles running, winded,
and finally slowing to call out
a Latin phrase from the mass—even as
the black wheels whirled faster, hurtling
headlong into our rain-drenched valley
where we'd lose sight of it for good, especially
those of us whose apple-filled pockets
the spoiled old geldings poked at.
Their giddiness in our hands—it was all
we could do to keep hold of the reins.

VOLUNTEER

I go around and turn the pages—the newest
news—for the paralytics on the porch.
At least the day isn't hot yet. So says
only a gleam in an old man's eye. A bee
zeroes in for the kill. I roll the ladies
to the shady side. No one wants word
of war. They go for a strangled baby on page 3,
continued on page 9, and everything all blue
and purple in between. *I'll show you hot,*
I could say, but I stick a straw between lips.
The stung one needs the first sip. Time to
re-pin my smock's ragged hem and repeat
what I reported yesterday, which no one
believes: *Those ants help the peonies blossom.*

THE APOPHATIC

How can it not be
about engine,
secret blaze behind
the wheels? How not about
this no-way-to-resist seeing
but one side or another
since the rails quite insist
& iron's so right, always
running off its own might.
How never about freightage
or the outdoor face
in the indoor light?
A yesteryear's pall
over the day at hand? Not
about the passings-by
of nailed-shut houses
& grouse setting sail
from a rusty swing?
How not me out of uniform,
out of a sleeper's berth,
bare & barely rising
atop smoke & so little air left
in the soft underbelly that soon
I shall meet—nay, embrace—
the hello-goodbye cloud.

WHEN HE SNAPS HIS FINGERS,

she'll no longer be aloft
on a thermal. She'll wake
and quit burning. Still be
arousable. Still wear pink anklets
and chew Chiclets. From here on
she'll nail the joke and not
crack herself up trying.
She'll no longer get
the sudden swells or shakes.
She'll let whoever's calling
leave a message.

What wakes her will leave
no mark. No echo. She'll rise
and walk through the cold
pre-dawn rooms, sifting among
tchotchkes, thinking all of it, everything's
been worth it . . . even these hours
on a stool bent over a bowl,
culling mealy walnuts
from moldy blue hulls.

NEST

We have a rental car, and thank you, no
we won't get out. We can see the animals
quite well from here.
                        We cinch up the lapbelts.
No way we'd turn back on a quarter-tank.

I have you and you have me,
            and we have, suddenly,
                        a slowed-down moment.

What **was** that waterfall doing?
        Oh, just exploding
                its veil of ice.

*　　*　　*

Cruise control, lipstick—we drive into the very nexus
        of the nest: scrappy twigs, string. And
                what?! —is that
                        *a **claw**?*
*So do we just drive **on**?*
        *Drive **through**?*

*　　*　　*

Pump and pay; sign and leave.
There was a day for the lake
and we could go around, spy
the rich folks' ballcaps. We could
smell our brethren. Never be
without the smell.

Coupon. Moon-pull.
Cash back and the needle north.

W for West. For went around. Some
trip. This traveling toward, this
only ever nearly approaching what
the barely alive
lived so hard to see.

ONE MUST DIVORCE ONESELF

: from the trouble. From the woman
walking out with the box of herself
from the man. That rattle
on the backseat. From
the man's ache as he lights
the stove and the stalled
whatwhatwhat begins
to stew. From the dog
wagging from one
to the other: who
who who
holds the leash
to the former life?

LEST YOU FORGET: CAKE NEVER COMES BEFORE THE PRAYERS

The corpse's wife, ex-wife, and girlfriend
wipe away each other's tears, blackening
white hankies. High heels in high weeds
the corpse had meant to mow, meant
to whack away under a highball sun.

While the half-brother spouts half-sentences
from a little red book, we teeter like black turtles
among gravestones. The mother's a prayer
under a veil on two stick feet. When you
get out of her way, you're in the brother's.

All morning we heard horrid news on a tape loop:
hour by hour another species going extinct.
Exquisite bugs and flowers—plucked
from foreign airs. Ah, my Liege, why is
your great pleasure our great sadness?

March on our mountain has been falsely
lionized: barely able to stand, let alone lick away
its purple blood sac. Lord, send in a real
wind. Send in a new wingéd whatever
for each what's-it expelled from the ethosphere.

When the silver cake knife rises like a groom
from the bride's velvet bed, the young cousins
edge closer. Sweet lambs in this late snow.
    Oh avalanche of advancing embraces,
            oh girls and boys of the blizzard,
                    the prick of pity stings, yes,
                            but it's gone in a flash.

BROUGHT TO US BY

It's gone in a flash! A day
or a life—all brought to us by:
5 a.m. mercies of tea, high
holy days, 10 p.m. illegal smokes
on a balcony. By the slipperiness
of our dead, and a streetlight
we'd shoot out if it weren't already shot.
By a black Mercedes grinding into
a wrong gear. By Out-of-the-City one day
and Into-It-Quite-Deeply the next.
By one's arrival as fireball, one's departure
as tapped-out beats on a telegraph. By
Nothing To Do vying with Everything
To Do. By special dispensations, no-guts
no-glory, Quaaludes, a ménage à trois,
and tales we mess up and pass on.
By stars loose against our tight flesh.
By endlessly rowing toward the dream's
last black harbor where the vertical spirit
slams against the horizontal sky.

Snowshoe Thompson & the Mail

The nibs   and cold blue fountains
    of the pen.   And no clear way
through the mountains.   Sixty-pound sack
    of moans, spells,   minds hollowed
to hysteria   and silk ribbons.

                                        Sadly
    the recipient   can't remember   exactly
the sender's lips   but senses   the slow press
    of her kiss   to the stamp.

                                    Two cents
for it,   and three for the scrivener.   Hard
    black marks   were all   she could sign
where instructed   at the bottom,   *love*

X

V. Cold Interiors

COLD INTERIORS

Rumpled, aquamarine pecker
of grapes. The strangeness of its wings
folded in—so it can be carted
in a shoebox away from a country
cashing out its skies. A voilà-fit
under the seat. But the fluttering inside
puts you in mind of your own live
burial. The splintering fingernails
you wished could gouge a crack
through the polished maple casket lid
your mother had wept over.

Remember the way her gold eyes
shown down? —Pricks of light
you steered the little boat by
in the fucked-up life of your dark.

Stateside, 1972

The judge ran down my list of offenses.
Christ, he said, and rubbed his eyes.
I told him I was pleading
ignorance. There wasn't anything
I knew anymore about the past.

Innocence you mean? He raised an eyebrow.
A matron brought water in small white cups.

Drink, I'm told. But I don't.
I won't. Outside, a church bell and a siren
sound at the same time. Crossing
into Canada, the two boys in my backseat
had been dressed as women. They're in
my charge, I was thinking, dreading
what might happen if they spoke.

Ignorance. I'd said it right
the first time. The wheel-hum
and icy switch-backing road. A glance
in the rearview mirror: gold earrings, gold wig,
and faces with a powdered finish. *Ignorance.*
I said it again. What was it
he couldn't understand?

DENIED YOUR HEAVEN, WE SHALL DENY YOU OURS

Wings, anyway, are, like brassieres, another cumbersome
strap-on. Our Tilt-A-Whirl Deluxe Delivery System
pops us in and out of the Downtroddens' Realm. Specters
inspecting. Have us a whim, and we're THERE—as, say,
third base your kid tramples racing home. Love that
foot in the face! Piggy toe in the eye. Love IT.

Plus, WE have a beach! And gill for gill, we can cavort
as fish among fishes. Can simultaneously eat and be eaten,
albeit often incurring the Holy Giggles, to which our
primo Gin Gimlets put a gentle halt. If we knew this
down there, Up Here we really Get It. All the rows
we have to hoe are hard, but—TILT!, and we're BACK
sowing the souls that are our merest everything. What
benignly falls on you? Some heathen's whim for rain.

LARDER

A seed of one thing confronts another
in the dark. Shameless date-stamped voices.
Fake-outs of studious poses. A light
snaps on—the plink of Daylight Savings.
I arrive to caress the dusty choices.

Hatchery of this for then and that for now.
On the package of Moon Flakes: the Sea
of Tranquility. Jugs, jars—balls to bat
toward the belly of infinity. Tap. Sniff.
My hand, the breaker of seals, bears down.

From the henceforth a hand withdraws.
Behind my back the numbers multiply.

NEGOTIABLE INSTRUMENTS

Work For Food, his sign says, so we
put him in our truck & truck him
to the building (condemned) & give him
a sledgehammer & a ham-on-rye & ditto
the same unto ourselves whose butt tattoos
read *Work Will Make Us Free* & we three
fall upon the struts & joists, we beat back
& swing low, we dig out & haul ass
so rubble is again as it's always been
the rule of the world, until he whom
we carried with us we may carry away
& re-feed and high five & bid adieu so he
may turn his sign at last to its flipside
that tells us to *Have a Blessed Day.*

CLICK ON ANY IMAGE TO ENLARGE HER

Mother of Plumpness, Mother
        of Swoon. Mother May-I, Madonna
                of our germ-free temple. Madre
                        under the orange yo-yo. Mother
                                Baby-step, Mother of
Dare Thee Not Strike but Lie Down and Let
        the Billy Clubs Lick Thy Wounds
                From the Last Time. Mother-face
                        lightning struck into an oak, a pizza,
                                an open sore. Mother-Flame Within
indivisible from the Fire Without.
        Mother of Bricks. Of Whistles.
                Of Hurry & Take the Kettle
                        From the Hearth, the Risen Bread
                        From the Oven. Mother of
Buttons. Of White Walls, White Floors.
        Veiled Mother. Maybe Mother. Mother of
                Mothers, please? Mother Pulse, Mother
                        Who's Sobbed Her Way into Our Arms.

CASTING THE WRONG SHADOWS

Odalisque and obelisk—two silos at dusk could not agree
on what dark shapes to shoot out behind themselves

over the rye fields. I dawdled, coloring in mauve toenails
on the nude. You stirred grays for the column.

We'd no sense of any grainy truth to be encased in the cast
shadows. We were all about duty . . . like fog lifting off a lake.

Plus the longest day of the year was coming
and we weren't ready: our shadows fell short.

We'd been so enamored of the paint, we'd wanted
to sip it. It seemed to seep up from a deep well.

Overhead: a murmuration of starlings. Nothing
is spared their physics or the cold fibrillating music

flooding down from their wings. Which was maybe why
we'd stopped for a kiss. Prolonging it, we provoked

a sudden sundown. Having so loved the world of us,
we let it set us apart from the work of us. Neither shadow

could hold a thing inside. Both were black gullets
with the wind blowing through. Yours was beautifully

diminished—distilled, diamondesque. Mine sat
with the moon in her mouth like a hostage gagged.

GONE TO GET MORE STUFF

May it be known we started out of town all
empathy and forbidden waltzes. How
thirst-free, how small our footprints
and carefree the first ransacking
of the forest. And dear page-turner,
how everywhere you found then
the nowhere-now snow owl.

May it be said we wanted only clearer
signage—for which turns and who
could take them, or when to dip
into our cache of corpses.

A brightness loomed ahead: white cliffs
at the edge of black days. So it passed
that we fell behind. Ghosts by the time
we embraced, and time had been so
of the essence. Would that we always were
such darlings of the future.

May it be told we packed our dream mule
and drove him around. We showed him
the whip but were loath to use it.
May it be clear we got close
to what we came for: phosphor
of the polestar, very hope,
very dawn, very near,
very now.

ABOUT THE AUTHOR

Nance Van Winckel is the author of seven other books of poetry, most recently *Pacific Walkers* (U. of Washington Press, 2014) and *Book of No Ledge* (Pleiades Press Visual Poetry Series, 2016). She's also published five books of fiction, including *Ever Yrs*, a novel in the form of a scrapbook (Twisted Road Publications, 2014) and *Boneland: Linked Stories* (U. of Oklahoma Press, 2013). She is on the faculties of Eastern Washington University's Inland Northwest Center for Writers and Vermont College of Fine Arts' MFA in Writing Program. The recipient of two NEA poetry fellowships, the Paterson Fiction Prize, Poetry Society of America's Gordon Barber Poetry Award, a Christopher Isherwood Fiction Fellowship, and three Pushcart Prizes, Nance lives with her husband Rik Nelson in Spokane, Washington.

ABOUT PACIFIC COAST POETRY SERIES

The Pacific Coast Poetry Series, an imprint of Beyond Baroque Books, was founded by poet Henry Morro in 2013, together with co-editor Suzanne Lummis and assistant editor Liz Camfiord. In 2015, the imprint produced its first book, the anthology edited by Suzanne Lummis and including 112 poets, *Wide Awake: Poets of Los Angeles and Beyond. Our Foreigner*, by Washington State poet Nance Van Winckel, is Pacific Coast Poetry Series' second publication.

ABOUT BEYOND BAROQUE BOOKS

The Beyond Baroque Foundation began in 1968 as an avant-garde poetry magazine called *Beyond Baroque*. Editor, publisher and founder George Drury Smith created the Beyond Baroque press in order to publish emerging, over-looked as well as established poets — especially those from Los Angeles. The Foundation began issuing perfect bound books and chapbooks in 1971. Titles include the first book from Los Angeles' recently named and first poet laureate, Eloise Klein Healy, works by Dennis Cooper, Amy Gerstler, Bill Mohr, Harry Northup, Holly Prado, and Wanda Coleman to name a few. The Foundation's current press, Beyond Baroque Books, was launched in 1998 by Fred Dewey. It has published fourteen books and several magazines featuring works by Jean-Luc Godard, Jack Hirschman, Diane di Prima, David Meltzer, and more. Beyond Baroque Books continues to unearth cult rarities as well as collections by noted performance poets, educators, and cultural leaders. Pacific Coast Poetry Series is a new imprint of Beyond Baroque Books.

ABOUT BEYOND BAROQUE

Beyond Baroque is one of the United States' leading independent Literary Arts Centers and public spaces dedicated to expanding the public's knowledge of poetry, literature and art through cultural events and community interaction. Founded in 1968, Beyond Baroque is based out of the original City Hall building in Venice, California. The Center offers a diverse variety of literary and arts programming including readings, workshops, new music and education. The building also houses a bookstore with the largest collection of new poetry books and CDs for sale and an archive that houses over 40,000 books, including small press and limited-edition publications, chronicling the history of poetry movements in Los Angeles and beyond. Through the years, Beyond Baroque has played muse to the Venice Beats, the burgeoning Punk movement and visiting scholars.

Beyond Baroque's mission is to advance the public awareness of and involvement in the literary arts; to provide a challenging program of events which promotes new work and diversity; to foster a place in the community for the exchange of challenging ideas and the nurturing of new work; to support writers through readings, workshops, books sales, publication, access to archived material and performance space; to encourage collaboration and cross-fertilization between writers and artists in multiple disciplines with the goal of producing mixed media art; to use the literary arts as a foundation for increasing education and literacy in our community.

Made in the USA
Charleston, SC
24 December 2016